SAND DUNES
OF THE
GREAT LAKES

PHOTOGRAPHS BY **C.J. ELFONT**   TEXT BY **EDNA A. ELFONT**

Sleeping Bear Press
121 South Main
P.O. Box 20
Chelsea, MI 48118

Sleeping Bear Ltd.
7 Medallion Place
Maidenhead, Berkshire
England

Printed and bound in Canada by Friesens, Altona, Manitoba.

10 9 8 7 6 5 4 3 2 1

Cataloging-in-Publication Data on file.

ISBN 1-886947-16-3

Title page photograph: *Silver Lake State Park*

Dedication

This book is dedicated to all those who have worked to help preserve the Great Lakes dunes.

Silver Lake State Park

Foreword

The coastal sand dune formations that border portions of the Great Lakes shoreline are the largest assemblage of freshwater dunes on Earth. With their towering sand cliffs, mounds of barren moonscape clusters, rolling wooded hills and lightly vegetated interdunal valleys, sand dunes are one of the most striking features on the landscape. Few, if any, areas in our region are more arresting than the dunes or attract more visitors.

It was this attraction that inspired C.J. and Edna Elfont to produce this first major portrait of Great Lakes sand dunes, which are the most fertile and complex dunes in the world. Much more than shifting hills of sand, the dunes possess a beauty found in no other environment. *Sand Dunes of the Great Lakes* provides a theater wherein closer observation allows you, the reader, to witness the eternal forces of water and wind ever building, ever tearing down. One need not be a scientist to see the beauty of the dunes, to sense the drama that is taking place, to feel the surge of some creative force beyond human understanding.

Just a generation ago, conservationists won the fight to preserve some of these dune areas for state and national parks before they were transformed into industrial or residential sites. Today, the book you hold in your hands offers further evidence that the sand dune ecosystem is a very special, fragile place—one that deserves our appreciation and protection as a truly unique global resource.

Richard Morscheck, Editor
Michigan Natural Resources Magazine

Grand Sable Dunes

PASSING
TIME IS SIMPLY
THE PERCEPTION OF THE
DISTANCE BETWEEN BEGINNINGS AND
ENDINGS.

Introduction

From the beginning of an event to its end, we are aware of intervals…the time between the start and end of a movie, between the beginning and end of a kiss, between hello and good-bye. How we perceive those intervals changes with our moods and perspective and is as different for each person as we are from one another. There are places, however, where beginnings and endings are measured only by the natural rhythms of day and night, by the changing seasons, or by the cycle of life itself. The sand dunes of the Great Lakes are such places.

In the less visited of the sand dunes, the staccato sensations that punctuate our daily lives are absent. Sound is muted and "events" are the wind stirring the dune grass, a monarch butterfly investigating a milkweed plant, or the arrival of a goldfinch seeking nesting material from a Pitcher's thistle. We have only to be observers in these unmanipulated corners of our world.

Wrought of glacial magic, the Great Lakes' dunes are the world's largest accumulation of dunes that border a body of fresh water. They are unique in both their origin and the multitude of environments

Pink Lady's Slipper

that exist upon them. They are irreplaceable because the forces that caused them to exist are long gone and are unlikely to ever return. Unlike New Mexico's White Sands or the dunes of the Sahara, the dunes of the Great Lakes are not simply vast accumulations of sand, devoid of water and color. They are endowed not only with stretches of uninterrupted sand, but with beaches bordering freshwater lakes, fields of grasses and wildflowers, mature forests, ponds, swamps, and rivers. The dunes of the Great Lakes are studies in contrasts. Dense beech-maple forests are but steps away from vast stretches of sand bearing little more than sparse patches of pioneer grass. Even the light is capricious, painting the landscape first in vibrant hues and then suddenly muting them with moody watercolors.

Their beauty is delicate, yet dramatic—places where change is the only certainty. Unlike their more desolate relatives, the movement of these dunes is limited to an area rarely over a half mile from shore. In the brief span of just the last hundred years, however, their movements have covered and uncovered forests and at least one town. And none is the same after their passage.

The dunes stretch along hundreds of miles of the southern and eastern Lake Michigan shoreline and extend to the northern lakeshore in the Upper Peninsula of Michigan. There are dunes on the eastern side of Lake Michigan, although these are smaller both in size and geographical distribution than the more well-known collection on the western Lake Michigan shoreline. There are also dunes along small areas on both the western, eastern and northern

Milkweed pod

edges of Lake Huron, the northern shore of Lake Erie, along the southern shore of Lake Superior, and the northern shore of Lake Ontario. Although Michigan has the largest and most extensive collection of dunes, Wisconsin, Indiana, Illinois and Ontario are all graced with their presence. The dunes must be seen from the top to appreciate the vistas, from the bottom to appreciate their size, and from afar to appreciate their imposing presence on the land.

This book is meant to be neither travelogue nor scientific treatise. It is simply one man's vision of a unique environment and one woman's attempt to tell what the images cannot.

Common Violet

Sleeping Bear Dunes National Lakeshore

Sleeping Bear Dunes National Lakeshore

THE ONE
PERFECT MOMENT
IN A STORM, IS THAT IN
WHICH A SHAFT OF LIGHT, SIGNALS ITS
DEMISE.

Grand Sable Dunes

Grand Sable Dunes

Ludington State Park

Geese of
Origami
Are silhouetted on
Canvas made incandescent by
Sunset.

Whitefish Dunes State Park

Sand Dune Drive near Eagle River

BORN OF
TIME, ICE, AND WIND,
THE SANDS SING OF ANCIENT
FORCES WHICH SHAPED OUR WORLD AND GAVE
THEM BIRTH.

It Began With Ice

In the far north, it grew cold and it snowed. The cold intensified and the snow deepened. Summer came and warmed the earth, but the sun could not melt all the winter's snow. What the sun could not melt changed into dense ice granules. Summer waned and again it snowed. Below the surface of the accumulating snow, the deeper layers melted under the weight of new snow and, with the deepening cold, refroze. The ice thickened and the pressure deformed the ice granules. The granules melted, refroze, and recrystallized, becoming ever more dense and compact. At the lower levels of the increasing mass of ice, recrystallization continued until the ice was as dense as ice can be. The transformation continued until it became "glacial ice", an ice so dense it is more like rock than it is like the ice cubes we put into drinks.

It took about ten thousand to fifteen thousand years to change what must have started as a continuous thin snow field into continental glaciers. Eventually glaciers formed that covered the Great Lakes with masses of ice up to one mile thick. When the ice was at its thickest, the bedrock of Hudson Bay lay more than two miles below the glacier's surface.

Spotted Coral Root

In the glacier's youth, when the ice reached about thirty feet deep and its mass was great enough, it began to move. And so these great aggregates of ice slid slowly south fed by more cold and more snow.

The masses of moving ice filled once green valleys, seeking the paths of least resistance. As the glaciers moved, they scraped and scoured the earth, trapping rocks, soil and anything else in their path. They moved only an average of a few thousand feet per year, so that it took four thousand years for a rock from the Arctic circle to reach the Great Lakes. Glaciers broadened valleys and deepened them into immense depressions that would eventually fill with glacial meltwaters to form the Great Lakes. These forces were so great that the basin of Lake Superior would eventually lay 700 feet below sea level.

Like mammoth earthmoving machines, the glaciers gouged rock from the terrain over which they passed. Once seized by the ice, rock was crushed and ground. Sometimes a glacier spat out massive boulders and sometimes it scattered about naught but pebbles. Ice was added at the north end of the glaciers so that everything trapped within was pushed farther and farther south. Boulders of ten feet or more in diameter and tons of rock debris eventually traveled many hundreds of miles.

Eventually the amount of new snow falling at the north end of the glaciers decreased, while the ice front in the south continued to melt. And so the glacier began its departure. Upon retreating, the glacier left great deposits of all it had engulfed. That retreat was neither complete nor final. Many periods of retreat and advance were to occur before their final departure from the Great Lakes area began. Each time a glacier's progress halted or began to retreat, it discharged its cargo of rock, gravel, sand and clay in great mounds called moraines. The forces of wind and water would eventually work their magic on these mounds of rock debris and create from them the Great Lakes' sand dunes.

As the ice began its first significant retreat about thirteen thousand years ago, the basins gouged by the ice filled with glacial meltwater. A complex lake was formed which continually grew as the glacier retreated. As the waters' depth increased, their waves pummeled the moraines that confined them. Then, as now, winds blew over the Great Lakes from the west. Picking up speed as they passed unimpeded over the lakes' surface, waves crashed against the unsorted mass of rocks, pebbles, gravel and clay that lay along the shore. The water tore anything from the moraines that it was strong enough to move. The heaviest rocks were pulled but a few inches towards the water, the lighter gravel a bit farther, and sand was carried out into the lake.

Not all the glacial melt formed the Great Lakes. Where the ice did not cut huge basins from the land, the waters from melting glaciers were channeled into streams and rivers. Cutting through the moraines over which they passed, the waters picked up much of the moraines' fine material. Moving rapidly, the water was able to hold in suspension all it had extracted from the moraines. The waters of those streams and rivers that found their way into the Great Lakes

Spotted Sandpiper

White-tailed Deer

slowed as they entered the massive body of water and deposited their burden of clay, sand and pebbles.

The water of the Great Lakes eventually found an outlet near the present city of Chicago and emptied into the Mississippi River. Later, melting ice opened another outlet farther north and the water drained through the eastern Great Lakes. As different outlets opened and deepened, the lakes dropped to progressively lower levels until they were even lower than they are now. During a period about 9,500 years ago, when drainage occurred across Ontario into the Champlain Sea, an estuary of the Atlantic Ocean, lake levels in Lake Michigan and Huron were at least 180 feet lower than they are today.

For between five hundred thousand and two million years, the glaciers sculpted and resculpted the land before they withdrew from the Great Lakes basin ten thousand years ago. It was not until the 1830's, however, that scientists began to study glaciation. Only then did we begin to understand the period called the "Ice Age" and the significance of glaciers and how they reshaped our part of the earth.

Four great continental ice sheets covered and then retreated from more than one-third of the earth's land surface. Nowhere else in the world, however, did the glaciers move as far south as they did in the Western Hemisphere. Of the four glaciers, evidence of the second and third glacial periods has only been found in traces (in Ohio and Indiana). It is the fourth and final that left the most evidence of its passage. Although the glaciers retreated from our corner of the world, they did not disappear from the face of the earth. To this day, the remains of the last ice sheet that once covered much of North America are still carving the land just west of Greenland on Baffin Island in the Eastern Arctic. This is where the glaciers were spawned and where they are likely to be reborn if conditions allow.

When the last of the ice sheets disappeared, the land, which had sunk under their weight, began to slowly rebound. Because the earth's continental land masses "float" on a layer of semi-molten rock, they are capable of moving up and down. The depth to which the continents sink increases when the weight of the overlying land mass increases. The buildup of continental ice sheets caused the land mass to increase so tremendously that the earth's crust sank as much as one-half mile under their weight. When the ice sheet broke up, the sluggish rock beneath it responded very slowly. Thus, while the melting ice deepened the lakes and formed new ones, the land was still rising, which decreased the number of outlet channels. So the water level kept increasing, but the rate at which the land rose exceeded it. So today, very old beaches and their accompanying dunes are found from sixty-five to six hundred feet above the present water levels.

The shape and area of the lakes continually changed over many years in response to the continued melting of retreating glaciers and the rebound of the land. For the past two thousand and five hundred years, there have been no changes in the geography of the Great Lakes that geologists consider significant. The rest of us, however, think of many of these changes as awesome. In the spring of 1996, the perfectly preserved remains of a freighter that went down in 1911 off South Manitou Island and which sand probably covered within three to four years of its sinking, suddenly became visible. In one winter, storm waves not only removed enough sand to reveal the ship, but also

Yellow-bellied Sapsucker

removed an immense portion of beach as well. It is estimated that in approximately five years, sand will make the ship invisible once more. Waves and storms still draw and redraw the shorelines, yet these kinds of events are very minor adjustments when contrasted with the phenomenal reshaping of the land as it occurred but a moment ago in our geological past.

Brown Creeper

Ludington State Park

Silver Lake State Park

Sleeping Bear Dunes National Lakeshore

THERE ARE
MOMENTS WHEN I
THINK CLOUDS MUST LIVE IN STILL
WATERS AND ARE REFLECTED IN
THE SKY.

Ludington State Park

Sand Reed Grass

The Pinery, Ontario, Canada

WITH THE
PERSISTENCE BORN
OF INFINITE TIME, THE
WATERS OF THE EARTH TRANSFORM ROCK
TO SAND.

Opposite: Silver Lake State Park

Ludington State Park

Ludington State Park

Silver Lake State Park

IF THE
WATERFALL IS
A ROAR, AND THE RAIN IS
CONVERSATION, THEN FOG IS A
WHISPER.

Grand Sable Dunes

Port Crescent State Park

Grand Sable Dunes

I KNOW,

WHEN DRY, IT SLIPS

THROUGH MY FINGERS LIKE RAIN,

BUT WET I CAN MOLD AND SHAPE IT.

IT WARMS

IN THE

SUN AND STAYS SO

LONG AFTER COOL WINDS BLOW.

IT STICKS TO MY SKIN, IS SMOOTH 'NEATH

MY FEET,

YET SCARS

ALL THINGS OVER

WHICH THE FIERCE WIND BLOWS IT.

I KNOW NOT WHERE IT'S FROM. THEY

CALL

IT "SAND".

Silver Lake State Park

Then There Was Sand

Ancient man may have used simple phrases to describe the mounds of granulated rock he found scattered about in his world. We are far from him in time and space, but our description of sand is no more complex. Even today, we define sand merely as "the more or less fine debris of rocks, consisting of small, loose grains". But sand in different locations is as unique as the humans that walk upon it.

Unlike the gypsum sand of White Sands, New Mexico or the calcite sand in Bermuda, the sand of the Great Lakes' coastal dunes slips through ones' fingers like granulated silk. It is millions of tiny, clear fragments of quartz crystals (9 of every 10 sand grains are quartz) that give this sand its smooth, sensual texture. Like rubbing your finger on the rim of a fine crystal goblet produces a clear tone, it is said that rubbing your bare feet along the band of wet sand just above the water's edge will do the same, and thus the expression "singing sands". It is thought that the friction between the quartz crystals and the moisture caused by the pressure of a foot produces the sound.

Trillium

The sand of the Great Lakes dunes is unique because its nature was defined in millennia past when great glaciers moved south from their Arctic origins and left their imprint on our world. Great Lakes sand came from the quartz-bearing rocks the glaciers churned up from the earth over which they passed. When the rocks were released from the frozen grip of their icy captors, they lay in massive heaps up to one thousand feet deep. These were rocks such as granite, sandstone, and conglomerate in which quartz was, and remains, the most abundant of all minerals. Because quartz does not chemically combine with other substances, the quartz that arrived so many thousands of years ago still exists today. Once formed, it is resistant to weathering, and is so hard that it is the most difficult of all minerals to destroy.

But forces beyond the glaciers were responsible for the transformation of the quartz-bearing rocks into sand. Water, the persistent reshaper of our world, was the force that freed the quartz from the rock of the glacial moraines in which it was bound. The waves of the ancient Great Lakes pounded against the moraines at the shore, wore down the rock, and carried the quartz and other materials into its depths as sand. Inland, rivers formed from melting glaciers eroded the moraines and carried more sand and pebbles toward the newly formed lakes. The sand fell onto the lake bottom as the particle-bearing water reached sixty feet in depth and lost its momentum. Once part of the lake bottom, the sand awaited the combination of events that would concentrate it and expose it to the fierce and ever-present wind.

Wind and water are forces in our world whose nature and effects are inexorably linked. Water is moved by wind, and winds are swayed by the presence and temperature of water. For water to move sand, it must first be moved. The huge temperature differences between the ancient lake waters and the shoreline, along with the vast open expanses of water, combined to produce persistent, high-velocity winds that gave tremendous power to the surging waters of the lake. Even now, the air cooled by the lake is drawn toward the warmer air overlying the land. The forces of these local winds are sufficient to set the water in motion. Where dunes are small, these were, and continue to be, the primary dune-building forces.

Once in motion, water has enough force to lift the granules of sand from the lake bottom and propel them towards the shore. The stronger the winds, the more forcefully the water moves. The more forcefully the water moves, the larger the particles it can pick up from the lake's bottom. During storms, the water may pull pebbles and even rocks from the lake bottom and hurl them onto the beach. Waves driven by the fiercest of storms may actually drag sand back into the lake depths.

Complex physical forces cause water to move in waves that bend as they reach shore so that waves strike the beach at an angle. The water at the end of the wave closest to shore slows as it is pushed along the beach and it deposits its burden of sand granules. If this were not so, the water might drag as much sand back into the lake as it carries to the beach. Shore currents continually move sand parallel to the shore. When these suddenly encounter a bay or a river entering the lake, they slow down in the face of the deeper, quieter mass of water and dispense their cargo of sand. Eventually, enough sand builds on the lake bottom to form a sand bar or spit. There is rarely enough sand on newly formed spits to build dunes, but

Sea Rocket

their sand is moved by water and wind to build and replenish the dunes along the nearby shore.

If the spits grow long enough, they can close off a bay, forming an inland lake such as Clark Lake near Sturgeon Bay, Wisconsin, Crystal Lake near Frankfort, Michigan and Silver Lake near Mears, Michigan. The events that produced these lakes occurred several thousand years ago when the water level of Lake Michigan was considerably higher than it is today. The dropping water levels enlarged the spits and added to the sand supply available for dune formation. Today, all these sites have active dunes of considerable size. Clark Lake's dunes are protected within Whitefish Dunes State Park in Wisconsin and Silver Lake's dunes within Silver Lake State Park in Michigan.

Once sand granules are deposited on a beach, the power of water is capable of binding them to each other for a while. Exposed to the air, however, it is not long before the water dries and the wind claims the sand for its own. Wind is the ultimate sand granule sorter. Fine sand (under one quarter of a millimeter in diameter) will begin to roll in a breeze of eight to twelve miles per hour. Grains up to one millimeter will not budge until a wind of over twenty miles per hour conquers their inertia. And, although strong winds of twenty-five to thirty-one miles per hour will move grains of one millimeter in diameter along the ground, only gales of thirty-nine to forty-six miles per hour can lift sand high into the air. Therefore, sand is mostly earth-bound, seldom getting more than a foot or two off the ground. Upon those shores of the Great Lakes exposed to fairly constant winds of moderate to strong intensity, sand grains of primarily one-quarter to one-half of a millimeter were deposited again and again. And so it came to be that, unlike other sands, the grains of this sand were sorted so that approximately eighty percent of them measure in this very narrow range. And while only fifteen percent of the grains are smaller, even fewer are larger than one millimeter.

Not only is the size of the sand grains of these coastal dunes exceptionally consistent, but most have a similar shape. As these millions of mini-rocks bounce along the earth's surface, they scour the ground over which they pass. But the grains themselves are not unscathed. They are abraded by the very rocks they abrade so that most become rounded. The wind is a persistent jeweler, slowly shaping each sand granule while using them to facet pebbles and even boulders.

Nowhere else in the world are there quartz dunes of the size and extent found around the Great Lakes, but nowhere else did ancient forces combine in just the same way. The massive glaciers, the immense bodies of water produced by their melt, the intense and constant wind, the powerful waves, the masses of pulverized rock the glaciers left behind, and the rebound of the land were all necessary ingredients in the recipe for the unique dunes of the Great Lakes.

Chipmunk

Point Betsie

Silver Lake State Park

THE MAN
WHO IS GOVERNED
BY PRIDE, WALKS IN THE SAND
TO SEE THE IMPRINT OF HIS OWN
FOOTSTEPS.
THE MAN
RULED BY EGO,
AVOIDS THE SAND, KNOWING
THE MARKS OF HIS PASSAGE ARE SOON
ERASED.
WISE MEN
WALK IN THE SAND,
WISHING THEIR STEPS WEIGHTLESS
SO AS NOT TO MAR THE SCULPTED
SURFACE.

Sleeping Bear Dunes National Lakeshore

Ludington State Park

Silver Lake State Park

Lag gravel at Silver Lake State Park

THE SAND
WEARS A REGAL
CLOAK BEARING PRECIOUS GEMS
FACETED AND SET IN PLACE BY
THE WIND.

Ludington State Park

ALONE
IS A STATE WHICH
IS OCCASIONALLY
INTERRUPTED BY MOMENTS WITH
A FRIEND.

Whitefish Dunes State Park

Silver Lake State Park

Warren Dunes State Park

CLOUDS ARE
BALLOONS THE WIND
BLOWS INTO CARTOON SHAPES
AND FLOATS IN THE SKY TO AMUSE
CHILDREN.

Silver Lake State Park

Grand Sable Dunes

Silver Lake State Park

Opposite: Sleeping Bear Dunes National Lakeshore

Silver Lake State Park

Indiana Dunes State Park

Grand Sable Dunes

ARE NOT
MOUNTAINS CONQUERED WITH FORCE,
PITONS, ROPE, AND CRAMPONS?
THEN HOW ARE THESE MOUNTAINS MOVED BY
THE WIND?

Mountains of Sand

*T*ime and glaciers passed, as did innumerable geological and climatic events that produced strong, persistent winds that swept unimpeded across the vast surface of the Great Lakes. The fierce winds plucked sand from the glaciers' moraines, and carried it until the elevated land masses across which the winds blew slowed their passage and captured their cargo of sand.

Ancient beaches and their dunes, left behind when the lake levels dropped and the land rebounded, are now far inland. Formed about thirteen thousand years ago when the glacial lake levels were approximately two hundred feet higher than they are today, these inland dunes have become all but obscured by plants. During a period about four thousand years ago, when the Great Lakes were interconnected, powerful wave action produced extensive flats backed by strong cliffs. It was primarily then that these younger and more phenomenal dunes of Lake Michigan's coasts were formed.

The winds still blow inland from the Great Lakes. And now, as then, the wind's captive sand returns earthward when a barrier slows the wind's passage. The barrier need not be formidable—a rock, a small mound of sand, even a tiny blade of grass will capture a few sand grains that can become the nucleus of a new dune. As sand builds upon sand, the wind pushes the grains to the crest of the growing mound, smoothing the side against which it presses, creating a gently graded incline. When the height of the mound reaches somewhere between three and ten feet, it is said to have become a dune.

The sand grains that reach the crest of the new dune once again become vulnerable to the wind that greedily recaptures them. Since the crest itself is a barrier that slows the wind, the grains are quickly released and they tumble down the dune's steep back slope. As more sand adds to the back slope, it creeps inland in the direction of the wind's course. More wind...more sand! The dune grows higher and its back slope becomes steeper. If dry and free of plant growth, the back slope never gets much steeper than thirty degrees, since dry, loose sand cannot sustain itself at a greater angle. Even the ripples we commonly see in the sand have a gradual slope on one side and a steeper one on the other, revealing the direction in which the wind was blowing when they were formed.

Dark Eyed Junko

When pushed by the wind, some sand grains simply slide and roll in a motion called "surface creep". But some grains, once pushed, violently collide with others. The grains being struck jump, skip or bounce into still more grains that are sent careening into motion. This chain reaction (called "saltation") accounts for about seventy-five percent of the sand grain movement in dunes.

Sand grains that become airborne strike others even harder because the wind impels them downward, adding force to their movement. When empowered by a strong wind, the sand moves with so much energy that the grains form a constant hazy zone a foot or two above the ground. The years of bouncing and battering endured by a sand grain are not without its toll. The smooth, sculpted surfaces of beach sand, created by the churning motion of the water, are destroyed by the time the sand grains reach their lofty position atop a high dune.

The dunes of the first ridge, immediately adjacent and parallel to the beach, are called foredunes. These are geological newborns and are usually low in height (thirty to fifty feet). As with all things natural, "usually" means there are exceptions. Foredunes in the Aral Dunes along Platte Bay in Sleeping Bear Dunes National Lakeshore rise more than one hundred feet above Lake Michigan. Foredunes are the wall between the beach and the rest of the land-based world. Because they stand facing the lake with nothing to protect them, the foredunes must bear the full fury of storms and are frequently undercut by waves. Only the hardiest of plants survive the unabated onslaught of the winds and somehow manage to grow on and stabilize the foredunes.

Pitcher's Thistle

Behind the linear ridges of the foredunes may be older, active dunes that can cover thousands of acres as they do at Ludington, Michigan. Amongst these are the high dunes—those that rise over one hundred feet.

Another dune form is the blowout. These are created as a result of the wind slowly tearing away at sand that plants have secured and so they exist only in humid coastal areas like the Great Lakes. (Few plants grow in the arid deserts of the world.) When conditions are extreme and even the strongest of pioneer plants die, the wind regains access to the raw sand. The sand in an area thus exposed is blown inland, covering other small plants and even trees. As these die, more and more sand is picked up by the wind, and the area devoid of vegetation broadens and deepens. The sand is continually blown inland, eventually forming a U-shaped dune ridge called a blowout. Some blowouts may eventually protrude inland for a half mile or more and may have a crest that towers more than two hundred and fifty feet above the water's edge. Seen from the lake's edge, these look like huge, deserted amphitheaters.

Dunes differ from each other in more than just size and location. A dune's shape is like a sculpture created by many artists all using different tools. It is determined by the direction and strength of the wind that forms it, the amount of sand available, the geological conditions that existed when it was formed, the amount of erosion it undergoes, and even the structure (plant or otherwise) over which it is formed. Constant winds tend to form regularly shaped dunes or uniform long ridges. Although potentially predictable, the symmetry of these parallel sand ridges is frequently punctuated, and sometimes obliterated, by blowouts. Winds that change direction tend to form irregular dunes. In rare cases, dune ridges may even lay perpendicular to the present shoreline, as are some in Ludington State Park in Michigan.

In contrast to beach dunes (those that lie at lake level), perched dunes lie on top of glacial moraines, often several hundred feet above lake level. Rebound of the earth's crust uplifted the land on which these dunes were first deposited. Today, perched dunes tower four hundred and fifty feet above Lake Michigan at Sleeping Bear Dunes National Lakeshore, while those at Grand Sable Dunes in Pictured Rocks National Lakeshore rise three hundred and eighty feet above Lake Superior. The sand that renews these dunes primarily comes from the upper layers of the glacial material upon which they rest. As the wind approaches the cliff of glacial debris upon which a perched dune may lie, it is forced upward so it only impacts the top one-third. The fingers of the wind pick the sand grains out from amongst the larger pebbles and rocks and carry them up the cliff face. When the time comes that all the sand is extracted, the cliff or bank is said to be "armored". Cut off from a fresh source of sand, the dunes above become comparatively stable. Only mighty storms with waves powerful enough to undercut the cliffs on which they perch, winds strong enough to reach the top of the bluffs, or the destructive activities of humans tend to affect these perched giants. Occasionally, the sand of a perched dune migrates off its plateau onto an adjacent lowland, isolating it farther from a source of sand, as at the Dune Climb in Sleeping Bear Dunes National Lakeshore.

Nothing about dunes is unchanging. How and when a Great Lakes dune will grow or move is dependent on almost every environmental and climatic condition. In today's world, the three primary forces that keep the wind from making a Sahara of the Great Lakes region are the land itself, water, and plants. The effect that the land mass has on the growth and movement of dunes is that the wind loses velocity very quickly as it crosses the land. Without strength, the wind cannot carry the sand, so dune growth and movement occur only in an area within one-half mile of the shoreline.

Water, that glacial gift in the form of rainfall and groundwater, determines how far dunes will wander and how much land mass they will cover. The abundant water in the Great Lakes states makes dunes less vulnerable to the wind than they are in arid climates. When wet, sand granules are loosely bound and weigh more, so only a very strong wind can lift them.

Sand Cherry in fall color

Great Blue Heron

The more important effect of the presence of water is how it changes the ability of a dune to support plant life. When water from rainfall, snow, or any other source seeps into the ground, it penetrates the soil and fills the pores in the subterranean rock. The water table is the area at the surface of the subterranean rock layer that is saturated with water. The higher the water table, the more easily plants grow. As the number of plants on a dune increases, its sand is less available to the wind.

Such a dune tends to be stationary unless the plants are disturbed. Plants act as barriers to the wind, slowing the sand-carrying breezes that pass over them. Sand accumulates amongst the plants, helping the dunes to grow. Anything that assists plant growth, therefore, ensures that dune growth will occur more quickly and with fewer interrupted periods.

It is the interaction between water and plants that accounts for why dunes, mere feet apart, may grow to very different heights. With the exception of foredunes, not all dunes, even those close to one another, support the same kind of plants. Different plants have differing abilities to access the water table. Those more capable of sending roots down to the water table grow more efficiently. The more efficiently they grow, the more sand they will capture and the higher the dune will grow. Because the underlying rock and sediments vary beneath neighboring dunes, even the height of the water table will vary from site to site. The ability of water to percolate through these subterranean layers will be different and so too will be the level of the water table.

The water table fluctuates in direct relationship with the lake level. When the lake level rises, vegetation thrives, thereby stabilizing existing dunes. When the water table drops, stabilizing vegetation may die, allowing the wind access to the sand once more. If the lake levels rise too far, storms may produce ferocious waves that erode the dunes rather than raise the water table to help plants grow. Over the last one hundred years, the Great Lakes dunes became increasingly stabilized. Recently, however, the eroding action of the higher lake levels seen in the mid-1980s reversed that process in many areas. There are so many factors that influence dune growth that, along Lake Michigan, the amount of growth of any one dune may vary from one to five feet per year.

If dunes are to grow, new sand must become available. Changing water levels in the Great Lakes may have a pronounced effect on the sand supply. Normally, the level of the water in the Great Lakes differs during the year by only one and one-half feet. This has little effect on the amount of sand. During the year, the wind spends most of its energy sorting and redistributing the sand already available. High lake levels produce fierce waves that scour sand from the lake's bottom or erode it from steep banks against which the waves are driven. Such powerful waves may cause cliffs to collapse, bringing down heavy rocks and the loose sand trapped around them. Even previously unexposed glacial deposits or older sand dunes may be eroded. Then, during low water periods, sand is deposited once more. During prolonged low water periods, beaches can be extended into the lake by over one hundred and fifty feet. Offshore bars emerge during low water and provide new sand from which new dunes may result. These actually help protect beaches by catching the sand that winter storms take from the beach. Were it not for the sandbars, the sand would find its way to the bottom of the lake, to be returned only when extreme conditions occurred. Trapped on the sandbar, even the gentle breezes of summer can carry the sand landward. Another source of new sand is from new shorelines. These are created when land that was depressed as much as one-half mile under the weight of the continental ice sheets rebounds and is exposed. (The northeastern edge of Lake Superior is still rising at a rate of twelve to twenty inches a century.)

And so the years pass and the elements alternately wreak havoc upon or rebuild the Great Lakes shorelines. Each new climatic condition contributes in its own way to the movement of sand and leaves its impact on the mountains of sand we call "dunes".

Grand Sable Dunes

THE GRASS
AND THE WIND ARE
TENACIOUS FOES, PLAYING
KING OF THE MOUNTAIN FOR A PRIZE
OF SAND.

The Pinery

Grand Sable Dunes

Whitefish Dunes State Park

SAID THE
MOUNTAIN, I WILL
CHANGE SO SLOWLY THAT NONE
WILL NOTICE AND PEOPLE WILL FEEL
SECURE.
SAID THE
SAND DUNE, I WILL
CHANGE WITH THE WIND SO
THAT ALL WILL SEE AND BE FILLED WITH
SURPRISE.

Silver Lake State Park

Grand Sable Dunes

Ludington State Park

Only
The dune flowers
Come to worship beneath
These desiccated cathedral
Spires.

Opposite: Sleeping Bear Dunes National Lakeshore

Pyramid Point, Sleeping Bear Dunes National Lakeshore

Ludington State Park

FROM 'NEATH
A MULTI-HUED
FAN OF CLOUD, THE SUN WINKS
AND TEASES ME WITH TOMORROW'S
PROMISE.

Ludington State Park

Sleeping Bear Dunes National Lakeshore

THE BLADES
OF MARRAM GRASS,
PROVIDE A SAFE HAVEN
FOR GRAINS OF SAND TORMENTED BY
THE WIND.

Of Beaches and Grasses

Beaches, to beach lovers, are playgrounds, each having a unique character and beauty. They are like magnets to most humans, causing us to run to the water's edge like so many lemmings. Once ensconced on a blanket or in a beach chair, many never venture beyond the beach's limits. The cool breeze, hot sun, silky sand, and blue water are all they seek. Some will stay into the evening when the light becomes kinder and the sand turns shades of mauve and gray.

But there is more than their aesthetic allure; the beaches of the Great Lakes are necessary to the continuing good health of the dunes. While a sandy beach a dune does not make, Great Lakes dunes die without one. Wherever there is a sandy beach, the wider it is, the greater the potential for the formation of large dunes. Along most of the Great Lakes' shorelines, the waves and currents bring the sand from the lake to the beach. But there are places where this no longer occurs. One such spot is the Lake Ontario beach of Sandbanks Provincial Park's West Lake bay barrier in Ontario. Here the sand no longer reaches the shore. Blocking the sand-bearing water are outcroppings of rock that reach from just offshore to almost three miles out, beyond which there is a drop to deep water. So the beach is mostly gravel, and behind it, the dunes are slowly disappearing.

Stroked tenderly by the gentle waves of summer, the beach must bear the brunt of the fierce, storm-driven waves between fall and spring. Those beaches fortunate enough to have an off-shore sand bar are afforded some protection from these destructive forces. The sand bars cause the waves to break farther out into the lake so they absorb the energy of waves and currents. For most beaches, the only protection the beach sand has in the winter is from the thick sheets of ice that crowd against the shore. If not for these, many beaches would disappear by spring. Just as the ice protects the beach from erosion, it also prevents any sand from being deposited. This, then, is a time of maintaining the *status quo.*

It is hard to imagine how water can move the sand at the lake's edge, because it appears so well packed. Actually, each grain is protected from its neighbor, as well as from capture by the wind, by a film of water. It is this film of water that allows the lake water access to each grain. Like a jeweler's hand, the constant motion of the water over these grains polishes them smooth.

Eventually, the sand granules arrive at a position beyond the high water mark. Once on this "middle beach" area, their liquid protection evaporates as the wind or the sun carries it away, making large quantities of sand available to the wind. Seen in summer through human eyes, the middle beach is heaven. We come equipped with towels, chairs, and flip-flops to protect us from the heat of the sand. Our umbrellas, T-shirts, and sun-screen protect us from the heat of the sun. Cool drinks prevent dehydration and food is always close at hand. A dip in the lake cools us during the day and sweat suits drive away the evening's chill. The plant and animal life on the beach see a very different place—one that is harsh and foreboding even in summer. The temperature of the sand can reach over one hundred degrees under the summer sun and the air at its surface can reach one hundred and thirty-five degrees. The reflective sand intensifies the sunlight and daytime heat, but sand quickly loses that heat, making some nights extremely cold. The constant wind and searing sun cause rapid dehydration, and the soil has only minute quantities of nutrients to support plant growth. The blowing sand abrades everything over which it passes and buries those things it cannot pass. Then there are the storm waves…. It takes a very special plant to survive in such a place. Survival is fleeting, however, because a Great Lakes winter brings subzero temperatures, terrible storms, and ice.

In the warmer months, those that do challenge the elements and grow in such a place frequently begin life amongst the pebbles, small rocks, tree fragments, and other debris that are deposited just beyond the high water level. In the shade of a driftwood fragment, a seed may find respite from the sun's heat, some protection from the wind, and a spot where decaying material may begin to accumulate, providing some minimal nutrients for growth. The plants that live in this harshest of environments are the gladiators of the plant world, taking on the fiercest of foes and surviving. They bear names appropriate for fighters, like sea rocket, seaside spurge and bugseed (or tumbleweed). They can sink their roots down to the water table and thus survive the severe desiccation of the sun and the instability of the sand. Although frequently washed by waves, sand does not retain much water. The sun and wind dry the surface so only the layer just below it stays damp. The water that does find its way below the surface drains quickly through the porous sand to the water table below. So each of the plants that manages survival on the beach must have some special adaptation for coping with the rugged world they call home. The sea rocket stores water in its leaves so that they actually look swollen, the seaside spurge lies flat to protect itself from the wind, and the bugseed has extremely narrow leaves so as little surface as possible is exposed to the sun. These robust plants do not actually stabilize the sand because they are few in number and nothing of their structure survives a Great Lakes' winter. They do play a role in the eventual formation of a dune, however, because any vegetation that protrudes from the sand

Little Blue Stem Grass

Silver Lake State Park

slows the wind and promotes deposition of sand.

On the upper beach, beyond the reach of waves, the dune grasses enter our story. These are the dune builders! The story of the Great Lakes dunes is as much a story of the grasses as it is of sand. No seasonal passersby are these. Marram, sand reed, and little bluestem grass arrive and stay if at all possible. They gain a foothold in any depression or tiny crevice that they can find. As the blades of grass thrust themselves into the sunlight and sand is captured at their bases, they form hillocks that dot the landscape, looking much like old straw dolls whose stuffing has escaped. Although small in size, the influence of these grasses on their environment is tremendous. Where the grasses grow, the temperature is more moderate, with fewer severe highs and lows. Because plants retain water, moisture does not evaporate from the ground as quickly or disappear through the sand into the groundwater. When plant leaves breathe, they slowly give off water into the air through a process called transpiration. The slow release of moisture, added to the shade afforded by the grasses, acts to cool the daytime temperatures during the growing season. This creates a less hostile environment in which other plants can grow and animals can live. As the grasses grow and die, they increase the nutrients in the soil, thereby paving the way for the growth of different plants with greater nutritional needs. The growth of the grasses also retards wind erosion and initiates sand deposition.

All other things being equal, if marram grass (American beach grass) did not exist, the dunes would not look as they do, persist as they do, or be as profuse as they are. Marram grass not only survives the brutal conditions on the dunes, but rapid sand burial invigorates it. When marram grass is transplanted to an area away from blowing sand, it often languishes and dies.

Marram grass has developed specialized associations with other living things to help overcome the deficiency of nutrients in the soil. Since beach plants grow in such limited numbers, their demise adds little organic matter to the porous sand, and what is added is quickly lost. Studies first done on the Lake Huron dunes showed that there is a soil fungus that assists dune grass by binding sand particles together which more efficiently captures water and nutrients. Consequently, plants that associate with the fungus grow better than plants without its assistance.

Marram grass has a waxy cover to protect it from the abrading winds. The real secret, however, to its growth and reproductive success in the hostile dune environment is beneath the surface of the sand. If marram grass had to depend on forming new plants from its seeds, it could not be as successful a survivor. The seeds must find a difficult-to-locate damp hollow or a protected site on the side of the dune away from the wind in order to germinate. New plants, however, are easily formed from rhizomes—special underground stems. As these stems grow outward from the main plant, they send new roots downward to find water and new shoots upward to form new plants. The fine hair-like roots can spread over a twenty-foot area, making dense mats that secure sand grains in place. Like hair clogging a drain, not only is sand trapped in this meshwork, so too are water and nutrients. In this way, the growth of marram grass provides for the needs of more fastidious plants that will succeed it. So effective is the complex root system that a dune secured by nothing but marram grass can grow to ten feet

Hairy Puccoon

Ludington State Park

tall. Rhizomes fragments torn away during storms or collapse of a dune can form a whole new plant on whatever site the wind chooses to leave it.

There is a specialized structure along the stem of this grass from which either a rhizome or an elongation of the stem can form. Called a node, it is separated from other nodes by a smooth portion of the stem called an internode. A plant may develop as many as one dozen internodes per year. The faster sand buries marram grass, the faster the internodes elongate. As they do, the leaves are pushed upward, enabling part of the plant to remain above the surface. Marram grass can survive sand burial of over three feet in a year. If the sand were to accumulate at this rate for several years in a row, however, even marram grass could not survive. The amount of sand that accumulates in a given year is dependent, at least in part, on the amount of plant growth. The faster and taller the marram grass grows, the faster sand is deposited. The more sand, the faster the marram grass grows, until finally the marram grass is buried or summer ends. Once winter arrives and the sand either partially or completely buries the dormant plants, there is less surface area to reduce wind flow and trap sand. Active sand deposition begins again only when new growth appears the following spring.

As well as marram grass survives the sun, the wind, and burial by sand, it does not fare well when other plant species begin to grow around it. This may occur because other plants interfere with the marram grass's elaborate root system. The marram grass participates in its own demise, however, because by the act of building a dune it changes the environment and nutrients in the soil so that other plants can grow.

Sand reed grass is the dominant dune builder where the wind is less intense and the rate of sand deposition lower or where erosion is slower. Although it too spreads by rhizomes, they are shorter than those of marram grass. Sand reed grass grows taller than marram grass, but it cannot elongate its stem to cope with sand burial. In the search for water, however, its roots plunge deeper into the ground. This allows it to efficiently protect a dune from erosion.

Although not a grass, another major player in the dune-building business is the cottonwood tree. Even though its seeds need low sheltered spots with some water in order to germinate, sometimes a footprint is sufficient refuge. Like the marram grass, they too can survive sand burial, growing faster than the sand can accumulate. While a cottonwood's central trunk may extend dozens of feet upward from the surface, new roots can grow from that part of the trunk that is nearest the surface. A cottonwood's roots grow aggressively downward for anchorage spreading over a wide area in a mirror image of its above-ground branches. These roots may travel as far as one hundred feet down seeking moisture. Passersby on the dune see what appears to be a small shrub but is really the tops of trees sixty feet tall and one hundred years old. Sometimes, all that rises from a barren dune is a cottonwood tree.

Ludington State Park

The early shape of a dune has much to do with the type of plant or structure upon which it formed. Marram grass grows aggressively upward and outward in clumps, so it typically builds broad dunes of moderate height. Those grasses which send off abundant lateral extensions favor the growth of low, broad dunes. Willows which also send off side shoots, but which grow higher than grasses, form broad dunes that can grow to considerable heights before sand overwhelms the trees. Cottonwoods stabilize dunes that are very high because these trees grow upward rapidly. Such dunes are narrow and steep, however, because the cottonwoods send off no lateral growth.

Legged sand dwellers also play a part in the growth of a dune. All the animal life that lives on the open beach or foredune has some adaptation that allows them to cope with the inhospitable environment. Several of these cope by digging into the sand to escape the sun. Digger wasps continually burrow, while burrowing wolf spiders live most of their lives in their underground homes. White tiger beetles have burrows that may be twelve inches deep. Each of these provides a path through which organic materials may be added to the top several inches of sand, converting it to soil in which plants with greater nutritional needs can grow.

On the unsheltered sands of the beach and the foredune, beauty appears in small things: the pattern of the imprint left by an insect's movement, the tracings made by a blade of grass, or the brightly colored patches of huge congregations of ladybugs, assembling on the beach for their late summer breeding season. Like the delicate purple of the sea rocket's flowers or the geometry of a grouping of colored stones at the water's edge, the harsh environment tends to make beautiful anything with colors that contrast with the sand, water, and sun.

Whitefish Dunes State Park

Silver Lake State Park

Sleeping Bear Dunes National Lakeshore

CANDLES,
LIT BY THE SUN,
FLICKER ON WICKS OF GRASS
TO HERALD THE ARRIVAL OF
EVENING.

Illinois Beach State Park

Grand Sable Dunes

GREEN IS
NOT A COLOR.
IT IS A RAINBOW HUED
GOWN THE FOREST WEARS TO GREET THE
EVENING.

Sleeping Bear Dunes National Lakeshore

Silver Lake State Park

Warren Dunes State Park

LIKE THE
BREEZE THROUGH DUNE GRASS
I'D NOT CHANGE THOSE I TOUCH,
JUST STIR THEM SO THEY'D RECALL MY
PASSING.

Pyramid Point

Saugatuck State Park

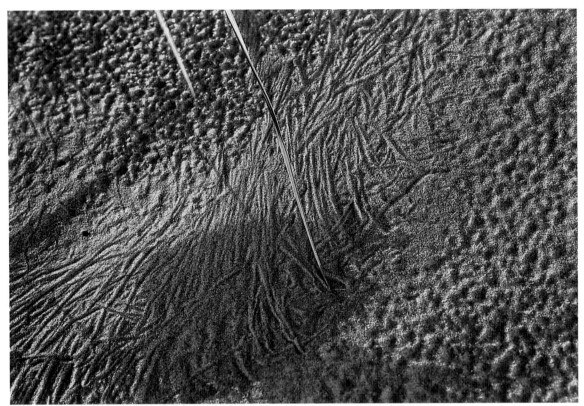

Silver Lake State Park

THE WIND
SPEAKS IN PHRASES
WRITTEN BY A STYLUS
OF MARRAM GRASS, ON A PARCHMENT
OF SAND.

Pyramid Point

Point Betsie

Silver Lake State Park

Ludington State Park

Pyramid Point

Point Betsie

BOUQUETS
OF YELLOW BLOOMS
MARK THE GRAVES OF TREES
TO HONOR THEIR VALIANT STRUGGLE
FOR LIFE.

Pictured Rocks National Lakeshore

Ludington State Park

AMONGST
THE GREAT LAKES' DUNES,
CLOUDS LIVE IN QUIET PONDS
COOLED BY SHADOW AND HIDDEN FROM
THE WIND.

Behind The Beach

The foredune is a wall separating a world of extremes of light and tone from one that is gentle and painted in watercolors. The transition is so dramatic that it is not unlike those described in children's stories—harsh reality magically transforms into delightful fantasy. Amongst the dunes, it is impossible to see beyond those that immediately surround you. Only wings would allow you to know the true scope of their expanse. Instead, your attention is drawn to the details wherein lies much beauty and variety. The variety comes from the multiplicity of environments that exists behind the foredune, each with its own complement of plants, animals, and birds..

Once behind and below the foredune, you are sheltered from the wind. Without its sound, others are amplified: the buzz and hum of insects, the songs of birds, even your own breathing. Without the wind, the heat reflected by the sand warms the air. The closer you get to the sand, the warmer the air. If you lie down, you may be able to replace the jacket you wore on the beach with a bathing suit.

The foredune is such a significant barrier to the wind, that its height affects the amount of sand added to, or removed from, the dunes behind it. The higher the foredune, the more it slows the wind, capturing more and more sand. As it grows higher, the wind that cannot pass it is forced up along its face. Reaching the peak of the foredune, the wind's high velocity tears away at the crest's vulnerable sand. This is the sand from which those dunes beyond the beach are replenished. The higher the foredune, the less sand for the dunes behind it and the lower they tend to be.

The dunes have protectors and predators. Added to the protection afforded by the foredune, from spring through autumn, growing plants also protect the sand. But when the savage winter winds arrive, the sand is particularly assailable. Frost, which forms on all wet surfaces, contributes to its vulnerability. The film of water that surrounds wet sand grains becomes frozen when the temperatures plunge. Ice crystals insinuate themselves between the grains and, as they grow, they push the grains apart. The strong winds desiccate the ice and capture the sand.

Unlike frost, snow is a protective blanket for the sand, shielding it from the raging winter blasts. The snow also protects plants from being torn away from the sand so they can regrow when the weather warms. But the wind prevents the snow from accumulating on all but protected areas, and the only protected areas are amongst the trees or immediately behind a dune.

Goat's Beard

The expanse behind the foredune is filled with seemingly ill-defined geometric patterns. Unless viewed from the air, the dunes that spread inland appear to have little symmetry. In reality, they are made up of long ridges running parallel to the shore. Each ridge, many of which were ancient shorelines, has its own complex of dunes, separated from the next by a valley of vegetation. Interrupting this repetitious pattern are the blowouts. These sandy horseshoes appear sporadically and unpredictably. Even if all the variables could be calculated, it would still be impossible to accurately predict when and where they might form or how large they might become. Once a blowout occurs, it dramatically affects the dunes behind and around it, because suddenly a large quantity of unsecured sand is available to the wind. All the variables that influence the movement of sand once again come into play.

Eastern Bluebird

A blowout can occur whenever a dune's protective vegetation is destroyed. It can begin with a seemingly insignificant event—a deep human footprint, a rivulet of water that makes a channel in the sand during a storm, or the death of a few plants when their roots are exposed to the sun. Although natural causes such as fires, windstorms, or plant diseases are historically to blame, human intervention has made a serious impact. Logging, mining, use of off-the-road vehicles, or simple human traffic is frequently the culprit.

The subtle differences in adjacent dunes, such as their shape, orientation of their slopes to the sun, or their height, can result in the plants that grow on them being very different from each another. Dunes of different shapes have sides with different angles, some steep and some gradual. On the steeper of the dune slopes, or where the wind is more intense, the plants and trees that flourish have elaborate root systems that anchor them in place. Since each side of a dune faces a different direction, it is therefore exposed to varying amounts of sunlight and wind. On those sides of dunes that face the sun, plants such as little bluestem grass that require direct sun will grow well. The higher a dune, the farther away from the water table is its top. Where dunes are small, on the lower portion of steep slopes, or in depressions created by blowouts, plants such as jack pine that need to be closer to the water table will prosper. Cedars, too, prefer sites closer to the water table. Since it is the type and density of the plants that influences the humidity, amount of shade (and therefore temperature), and the kind of nutrients added to the soil, anything that affects the plants changes the environmental conditions in their immediate area, creating microclimates. As time goes on, each microclimate may see the succession of different plant species. In addition, different microclimates provide habitats that appeal to different animals, so that often the types of birds, insects, amphibians, and small mammals vary from site to site.

The existence of microclimates provides the setting for what are some of the rarest assemblages of plants. One may find plants usually seen in the South, such as prickly pear cactus, black gum, papaw, and tulip trees in the same area with northern varieties such as hemlock, Canada yew, and white pine. It is believed that some of the northern wildflowers like bearberry and the evergreen, Prince's pine (pipsissewa), were originally transported south by the glaciers.

The lakes themselves also influence what plants can grow nearby. Because the Great Lakes are so large, they warm slowly in spring. This keeps the immediate land areas cool for an extended period of time. Plant buds will not open in cool temperatures. Since the area is prone to sudden spring frosts, buds do not open until all possibility of frost has passed. Frost kills many species, but late budding protects them. In the fall, the water is slow to lose its summer warmth, so the growing season on the nearby shores is extended.

The presence of the myriad of tiny yet different environments results in an unusually large number of plant species occupying a comparatively small geographic area. In the fourteen thousand acres that constitute Indiana Dunes National Lakeshore, 1,445 species of plants exist. Only two national parks have more, and each of these has over one half million acres of land. The Great Smoky Mountains has 1,485 different plant species and the Grand Canyon has 1,474.

Black-wing Damselfly

In few other places are the interrelationships of plants, animals, and the natural elements so obvious even to the casual observer. Consider the effect of swallows on erosion. After the summer, when vegetation dies or becomes dormant, the sand is less protected from erosion by the strong winds that follow. These winds scour the dune slopes that face them. Sometimes the effect is so intense that they create near-vertical dune faces. Bank swallows love making their nests in such vertical slopes, excavating their burrows up to three feet deep into the dune bank. When spring comes, they nest in colonies that can number a hundred pairs or more. Their burrowing may eventually undermine a steep slope, causing it to collapse during the winter following their departure. This destroys a part of the dune, freeing the sand to be carried away by the wind.

Some of what makes up the dune environment in those areas just beyond the foredune has more to do with water than with sand. It is the presence of water in pools, rivers and creeks, swamps, marshes, and bogs that seems to amaze newcomers to the dunes, but dunes and water are not mutually exclusive. The tranquillity of a pool amongst the dunes is in sharp contrast to the manner in which it is formed. When the wind is especially violent, it may carve a channel between dunes and scoop out the sand all the way down to the water table. As the water slowly filters up, it forms a pool. Many of these are transitory and may change dramatically from day to day. As the amount of evaporation, rain, or wind changes, so too will the depth of the pool. No landmarks these! What might be a large pond one week may have totally disappeared the next. Plants that are found nowhere else in the dunes thrive here. Essentially, each pond has its own microclimate and, certainly, its own beauty. Added to the flowers are the reflections, the footprints of the mammals and birds that come to drink, a floating feather, a broken eggshell. These are places of delicate shapes and colors—places to be savored because of their transitory nature.

One of the wonders of the dunes is the large number of orchids that may suddenly bloom in certain seasons of the year. Often thought of as delicate flowers that flourish in only the most protected areas, orchids actually thrive in conditions that are continuously, but mildly, disturbed. One such "mild" disturbance is the blowing sand endured by plants living amongst, or in areas bordering, dunes. Also, some orchid species are more dependent on the high acidity of soil than on how much water it holds. Such orchids flourish on dunes and even rock ledges. Orchids fare well in areas with few other plants because they do not tolerate competition for root space or sunlight. And so the dunes are graced with nodding Ladies'-tresses, Dragon's-mouth, Pink grass, Adder's-mouth, Yellow and Showy Lady's-slipper, Spotted Coral-root, and more.

Rivers and creeks that run through the dunes act as natural boundaries for the sand. The waters help

erode rock and bring new sand to the lakes that may eventually find its way onto a dune. Streams swell in spring, deepen their channels, and undercut the sand banks that collapse, adding more sand to be carried into the lake. This continues until often sand blocks the stream's outlet by summer's end. Winter storm activity moves much of the summer accumulations out into the lake.

Choke Cherry shrub

Numerous rivers and streams that once ran over ancient glacial moraines still run over their remnants. But this is not forever. When the streams finally cut down to bedrock, as they have near Sandbanks Provincial Park in Ontario, they no longer carry sand that can contribute to dune formation.

Water is found in many forms amidst the dunes, even as swamps and bogs. Like the dunes, they too have glacial origins. Some swamps were formed when sand spits closed off the entrance to a bay. The impounded waters formed a lake, and over centuries, many of these filled with decayed material. As the acidity of the water increased, the plant life changed. The vegetation continually filled in from the shore, occupying space that once held open water. Although swamps usually have some drainage, it is limited. In contrast to plants on the dunes, around ponds or even beside streams, white cedar, mosses, and ferns dominate the plant life in these areas.

The birth of a bog can be traced to a time over ten thousand years ago when a retreating glacier marooned a massive ice chunk in a bowl-shaped depression. As the region warmed, the ice melted, forming a bowl-shaped lake called a "kettle hole lake". Isolated as these are from streams or underground springs, vegetation eventually fills them and dramatically changes the acidity of the water. Aquatic plants such as cattails and rushes are the first to grow, then floating plants such as lily pads and duckweed. As the plants die, they decay and form a mass of floating peat upon which sponge-like sphagnum moss will grow. Even though the floating mat can support the weight of trees, it trembles and shakes underfoot with every step a person takes. These floating gardens are home to an assortment of insect-consuming plants and some marvelous orchids.

In the patchwork of environments that spread between the foredune and the oldest dune ridges, all things are possible. No two visits to this area of the dunes are exactly the same, and therein lies the fascination. There are thousands of images that are brought to mind when recalling one's visits. The images contained within this book are meant to bring all who leaf through its pages some pieces of this montage.

Port Crescent State Park

IF IT
WERE IMPORTANT
TO SEPARATE THE REAL
AND ITS IMAGE, WOULD REFLECTIONS
EXIST?

Kohler-Andrae State Park

Warren Dunes State Park

Silver Lake State Park

Ludington State Park

The Pinery

AUTUMN
TAKES VAN GOGH'S BRUSH
AND PAINTS ITS IMPRESSIONS
OF BIRCH TREES UPON THE WATER'S
SURFACE.

Grand Sable Dunes

Saugatuck Dunes State Park

Sleeping Bear Dunes National Lakeshore

IN THE
MEMORY OF
FORESTS LONG GONE, THE SAND
STRIPS TREES OF ALL THAT LIVES AND
LEAVES
MUMMIES.

Ludington State Park

Those who
Think others see
Them through a microscope
Chase perfection they can never
Achieve.
Those who
Wish to be seen
Through rose-colored glasses,
Want to be perceived as more than
They are.
Those who
Think the world sees
Them through a fish-eye lens,
Fear their image is distorted
And warped.
But some
Are unconcerned.
They have learned that they are
Seen by others only through a
Mirror.

Brevort River

Sand Dune Drive near Eagle River

JUST A
MOMENT OFF GUARD
AND THE SAND, CAPTURED BY
THE TREES OF THE FOREST, IS FREE
AGAIN.

The Forest: Final But Not Forever

As dune ridge is added to dune ridge, the breadth of the area over which the wind moves sand expands. Years, and finally centuries, pass and vegetation becomes more dense on the back dunes— dense enough to be called forests. These tree-crowned dunes are the final barrier to the sand's progress and may come to tower over all the dunes that separate them from the Great Lake.

The transition from dunes to forest is sometimes so abrupt that white dune sand spills onto the sable brown floor of the forest's edge. As you enter the forest from the dunes, there is a dramatic change in the brightness of the light and the temperature. There can easily be ten degrees difference between the forest and its surroundings. The rustle of dune grass quickly gives way to the muted sounds of the woods. The green of these woods is more like a rainbow of colors than a single hue. The contrast between the woods and the sand beyond makes a dune's forest seem especially green, lush, and, in spring and early summer, luxuriant with wildflowers. The tranquillity of these green oases is enveloping. Perhaps knowing what must have transpired to transform the harsh environment of the open dunes to a place of subdued light and quiet spectacles intensifies this feeling.

Monarch Butterfly

Cool green forests growing on sand dunes may seem an enigma. But it is easy to understand when one considers the millions of plants that must grow and die before the sand is transformed to soil rich enough to support a forest's growth. As plants die, their organic matter accumulates in depressions in the sand where the scouring wind will not remove it. The presence of this organic matter increases the capacity of the soil to retain nutrients. Trees that need vast nutrient supplies, water, and a stable substrate develop on only the oldest and most protected of the back dunes.

It takes approximately one thousand years for the sparse plant life on the nutrient-poor sand of the beach and foredune of a Great Lakes dune to be replaced with the trees of a climax forest (one in which the trees appear, grow and reproduce year after year, and are no longer replaced by other species). The most striking changes in plant life occur in the first few hundred years. Yet it takes several hundred more for the soil to gain the vast quantities of moisture and nutrients needed by beech and maple trees, the classic climax forest inhabitants. Although these forests exist in a number of dune areas on Michigan's coasts, many of the dunes of Illinois, Indiana, Wisconsin and most of Ontario have yet to develop the nutrients necessary to support the growth of beech and maple trees. In these places, the black oak forest is the highest stage of succession reached.

A climax forest's beginnings can be traced to the first sea rocket that took root on the bare sand beach, but its first "tree" predecessor is the cottonwood. On the dunes, cottonwoods rarely occur in groups large enough to provide widespread shade, so they never create an environment that in any way resembles a forest. One of the next trees to arrive on the dune is the jack pine. Once the foredune inhabitants have enriched the soil and a dune field has been created so the wind is reduced, the jack pine can flourish. These pioneers are robust enough to persist even on the dune slopes facing the wind and on the crests of dunes. Even in porous, sandy soil where the water rapidly percolates through it, jack pines thrive. Their deep tap roots and wide-spreading lateral roots seek out enough water to support a crown whose thick needles are designed to minimize water loss. Jack pines often serve as the buffer between the foredunes and oak or beech-maple forests, cutting the wind to which the hardwoods are more vulnerable.

Where jack pines grow, so too does bearberry. This original inhabitant of more northern climes spreads by sending new shoots from underground runners. But the bearberry only grows where it is protected from sand burial, because it is not capable of rapid growth. The jack pine is an excellent sand stabilizer and is thus an effective bodyguard for the bearberry. This protective relationship goes two ways. Although the seeds of jack pines sprout quickly, they must be given some respite from the wind. The bearberry provides just enough ground cover to protect the embryonic jack pines.

Once the jack pines have taken hold, wildflowers and shrubs that require the shade the pines provide begin to grow. Each of these contributes additional nutrients to the soil until the humus is rich enough to support the oaks and, in some locations, the hickories that will be the jack pines' successors. Oaks are more shade-tolerant than jack pines, so as the amount of light available to young

Monarch Caterpillar

Tufted Titmouse

trees diminishes, the growth of oak trees is favored.

The bark of these trees is thick and fire-resistant. Also, the roots can remain alive almost indefinitely even if the stem is killed. The underground system sends up generation after generation of sprouts, ensuring the dominance of oaks in drier sites. Because warm, dry conditions produce periodic fires, both jack pines and oaks have adapted by sprouting vigorously after fires, ensuring their ability to persist in this environment.

As humus and moisture increase, the frequency of fire is reduced, allowing beech and maple to grow. Where fires occur, beech and maple will not succeed, because both are extremely fire-intolerant due to thin bark near their bases and shallow roots. In the ever-deepening shade of mature trees, young beech and maple begin to dominate. Slow-growing, but very long-lived, young trees can persist for many years in the dense shade that exists under the canopy of leaves typical of mature forests. As the beech and maple mature, the shade they provide is extremely dense, favoring the growth of their offspring.

In many isolated places within these forests the smooth silvery bark of the beech stands in sharp contrast to the dark, jagged bark of the hemlock. Hemlock also thrives in cool, moist soils where the forest canopy allows little light penetration. These trees grow in small groups because, once established, they create their own microenvironment. Their needles are strewn on the forest floor to slowly decay. As they do, they produce strong acids that pull minerals and nutrients out of the soil, making it unfit for the growth of other plants, including their own seedlings. In addition, the roots of the hemlock pull water from the soil, and the large trees cast a deep, growth-inhibiting shade. The wind must spread the seeds of mature trees to distant locations, because survival near a parent tree is unlikely.

In the Indiana Dunes, where black oak dominates even on the oldest dune ridges, a beech-maple forest may never exist, for the black oak, like the hemlock, creates a microenvironment. Unlike the hemlock, the environment it creates does not prevent its progeny from flourishing, rather the environment allows only young black oaks to thrive. The growth of black oak allows nutrients not needed for their growth to leach away, leaving a soil too poor in nutrients to sustain a beech-maple forest.

The beech-maple forest, however, is the climax forest in many of the dune areas in Michigan. In the summer, the shade is so dense that only plants able to tolerate low light levels thrive beneath this canopy. But, oh!...the wildflowers. Many of the flowers bloom in the early spring before leaves appear on the trees. There is the threatened, very tiny Ram's-head Lady's-slipper that blooms for a maximum of one week in the cool months of the year. However, if pollinated within that time, a hormone reaction occurs which causes the bloom to droop. Here too are magnificent white trillium that must be six years old before they produce any flowers. The wildflowers that make dune forests the very special places they are are too numerous to list. Some are delicate and pale, some large and showy, but every one contributes its unique presence to produce an environment long remembered by any visitor.

Jack-in-the-Pulpit

Forests are the best protection for dunes because, even in winter, they effectively prevent wind damage. Even when the leaves are gone, the areas with a continuous canopy and high tree density cause the wind speed at ground level to be minimal. Also, any snow that penetrates the canopy and accumulates melts slowly in spring because of the deep shadows. This keeps the ground moist and provides an ideal bed for the growth of shrubs, ferns, and moss that further stabilize the soil.

In the last one hundred years, forested areas have increased, and the dunes have become increasingly stabilized. But every now and then, the stabilizing vegetation is destroyed and the sand is freed again. The initiating forces for such a release are as numerous as the factors that originally caused the sand to become stabilized. When the wind prevails, the grasses and trees give way, forming blowouts—great, sandy gashes that slice into otherwise green hills. As the sand is blown inland, forests formed many centuries before may become buried. The inland march of the sand, however, is limited by the wind's loss of force as it passes over the land. Also limiting the progress of a blowout is that wind erosion of the sand brings its surface closer to the water table. Thus, plants have easier access to water for more rapid growth. This enables new plants to restabilize the sand, so no further inland erosion occurs. Such a restabilization can occur in time to save a forest or a structure, but not always. The blowout between the Gillette Sand Dune Visitor Center at Hoffmaster State Park and Lake Michigan is one hundred and eighty feet high and, although restabilized, its crest lies within a few hundred yards of the building.

Occasionally the sand covers trees only to uncover them once more as it moves beyond. Trees so reclaimed, however, are mere skeletons, stripped of every living cell by the moving sand. These ghost trees exist amongst many of the Great Lakes dunes.

There have been places where logging destroyed the sand dunes' protective trees, with dire effects. The dunes at Sandbanks Provincial Park were once close to the shore of Lake Ontario and were eighty to one hundred feet high and heavily treed. After 1783, when the area was first settled, the land was cleared and logged. It was not long before the sand began to aggressively move. It is estimated that it moved one hundred and fifty feet in eight years and sand was blown inland for two miles. Whatever forest existed on the dunes behind those that had been cleared was gone. In 1915, a brick factory opened in the area but was abandoned seven years later because the sand could not be kept out. A 1991 study of the area stated that "…if the rate of movement of the back dunes continues as it has over the past two hundred years, within the next two hundred years, the dunes will almost entirely disappear into West Lake." Another place engulfed by sand turned loose to the wind after excessive logging is the town of Singapore on Michigan's west coast. Although mostly abandoned by 1875 after the timber ran out, the remaining buildings were already partly buried by 1883. By 1892, the last remaining house was vacated. The family that lived there had already moved to the second floor to escape the sand, but left when the sand began to run in the chimney tops.

That sand will move and dunes will change is certain. What form that change will take should never be under our control or we risk giving up the fun of being surprised. Amongst the protected dunes, we can take pleasure in a unique environment we neither created nor manipulate. The pleasures are many: the silent ballet of marram grass shadows on the sand, the shriek of hawks soaring on thermals over towering dunes, and the feel of warm beach sand as it slips across your fingers. We must be careful to preserve those places where we can go to reaffirm our place in the natural order of things, where we fit in but do not intrude.

Green-headed Cone Flower

Sleeping Bear Dunes National Lakeshore

Opposite: P.J. Hoffmaster State Park

Silver Lake State Park

Pyramid Point

—⋯—

STANDING
ON A DUNE CLIFF
IN THE FOG, ONE OF THREE
TURNED BACK, FOR HE SAID THERE WAS NOTHING
TO SEE.
ANOTHER
PAUSED A WHILE,
BUT LEFT SAYING THE FOG
WOULD NOT CLEAR AND IT WAS TOO HARD
TO SEE.
THE LAST
STAYED TO WATCH WHILE
GENIES OF LUCENT MIST
PLAYED AMONGST THE TREES AND THE WOOD
LILIES.

—⋯—

Saugatuck Dunes State Park

Sleeping Bear Dunes National Lakeshore

NAUGHT BUT
A BIRD'S SONG OR
SPLINTER OF LIGHT CAN BREACH
THE TIMELESS CANOPY OF THE
FOREST.

Point Betsie

Muskegon State Park

MEADOWS
HIDE THE PLACE WHERE
CATERPILLARS SING AND
DAISIES FLY AND OUR CHILDHOOD DREAMS
REPOSE.

Silver Lake State Park

Pyramid Point

WHEN THE
END OF A PATH
IS SHEATHED IN FOG, I AM
TANTALIZED BY WHAT MAY LAY JUST
BEYOND.

Silver Lake State Park

Acknowledgments

We would like to thank all those who gave us their time, information and assistance, without which this book could not have been completed. We extend special thanks to Richard Morscheck, editor of *Michigan Natural Resources Magazine*; Elizabeth Brockwell-Tillman, park interpreter, P.J. Hoffmaster State Park; Jane Law, PhD, University of Waterloo, Waterloo, Ontario; and Nancy McDonald, editor, *The American Cottage Gardner*, Grand Marias, Michigan. As well, we are especially grateful to the staff at all of the parks we visited as we explored the dunes of the Great Lakes.